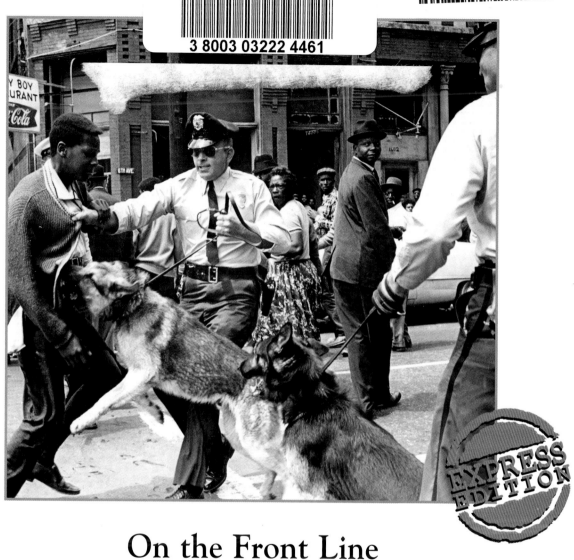

EXPRESS EDITION

On the Front Line

STRUGGLING FOR CIVIL RIGHTS

Stephanie Fitzgerald

Raintree

www.raintreepublishers.co.uk
Visit our website to find out more information about **Raintree** books.

To order:
☎ Phone 44 (0) 1865 888113
▤ Send a fax to 44 (0) 1865 314091
▢ Visit the Raintree Bookshop at **www.raintreepublishers.co.uk** to browse our catalogue and order online.

First published in Great Britain by Raintree,
Halley Court, Jordan Hill, Oxford OX2 8EJ,
part of Harcourt Education.
Raintree is a registered trademark of
Harcourt Education Ltd.

Produced for Raintree Publishers by Discovery Books Ltd
Editorial: Kathryn Walker, Juliet Smith, and Daniel Nunn
Design: Rob Norridge and Michelle Lisseter
Expert reader: David Downing
Picture Research: Amy Sparks
Project Manager: Juliet Smith
Production: Duncan Gilbert
Printed and bound in China by South China
Printing Company Ltd
Originated by Dot Gradations Ltd

ISBN 1 406 20244 4 (hardback)
10 09 08 07 06
10 9 8 7 6 5 4 3 2 1

ISBN 1 406 20251 7 (paperback)
10 09 08 07 06
10 9 8 7 6 5 4 3 2 1

British Library Cataloguing in Publication Data
Fitzgerald, Stephanie
  Struggling for Civil Rights. – Differentiated ed. –
(Freestyle express. On the front line)
  1. Civil rights – United States – History – 20th century –
Juvenile literature 2. Civil rights demonstrations – United
States – History – 20th century – Juvenile literature
  I. Title
  323
A full catalogue record for this book is available
from the British Library.

This levelled text is a version of *Freestyle:
On the Front Line: Struggling for Civil Rights*

Original edition produced by White-Thomson Publishing
Ltd, Bridgewater Business Centre, 210 High Street, Lewes
BN7 2NH.

Acknowledgements
The publishers would like to thank the following for
permission to reproduce photographs:
AKG pp. **6, 9, 15, 23, 25**; Corbis pp. **4, 7, 8, 11, 12, 13, 14,
16, 17, 20, 22, 26, 31, 32, 33, 34(l), 34(r), 35, 37(r), 38, 41**;
Getty Images pp. **10, 21, 39, 40**; Popperfoto pp. **19, 30, 36**;
Topfoto pp. **1, 24, 27, 28, 29, 37(l)**.

Cover photograph showing a man being arrested during a
demonstration by the Poor People's Campaign at the
Supreme Court in May 1968 reproduced with the
permission of Corbis.

Map on p. **18** by Jillian Luff.

Source notes: p. **18** Quote from James Farmer taken from
The Civil Rights Movement (Facts on File 1995) by Charles
Patterson; p. **23** Quote from Martin Luther King taken from
*We Shall Overcome: The History of the American Civil
Rights Movement* by Reggie Finlayson and from the *Eyes on
the Prize* documentary series.

Every effort has been made to contact copyright holders of
any material reproduced in this book. Any omissions will be
rectified in subsequent printings if notice is given to the
publishers.

The paper used to print this book comes from sustainable
resources.

Disclaimer
All the Internet addresses (URLs) given in this book were
valid at the time of going to press. However, due to the
dynamic nature of the Internet, some addresses may have
changed, or sites may have changed or ceased to exist since
publication. While the author and Publishers regret any
inconvenience this may cause readers, no responsibility for
any such changes can be accepted by either the author or
the Publishers.

CONTENTS

Any words appearing in the text in bold, **like this**, are explained in the glossary. You can also look out for them in the Word Bank box at the bottom of each page.

AN HISTORIC BUS RIDE

Fighting for equality

Black people in the United States wanted the same rights as white people. **Protesters** fought to change the laws. After a hard fight, the laws were changed. But changing the way white people felt about black people was even harder.

In the early 1950s, the southern United States had special laws to enforce **segregation**. Segregation meant keeping black and white people separate and unequal.

On buses, black people were not allowed to sit in the same rows as white people. Blacks sat at the back. Whites sat at the front. If all the seats at the front were filled, blacks had to give up their seats at the back to whites.

Black protester Rosa Parks walks to jail with her solicitor, Charles Langford (far right). She had been arrested for not giving up her bus seat to a white man. ➡

Word Bank   segregation   keeping black people and white people separate

Rosa Parks makes a stand

On 1 December 1955, a black woman called Rosa Parks was sitting on a bus. The driver told everyone in Parks's row to get up so a white man could sit down. Parks said no. The driver called the police and Parks went to jail.

This was just one example of the terrible way blacks were treated in the southern United States. Parks's action made many others want to change things.

Find out later

Why were these people protesting?

Where and when did Martin Luther King Jr make his famous "I Have a Dream" speech?

Who made the phrase "**black power**" popular?

protester someone who shows disagreement through organized action, such as a march or a sit-in

SLAVERY AND FREEDOM

Hundreds of years ago, black people were taken to the United States as slaves. Some had been taken by force from their homes in Africa. Others had been sold by their enemies.

Slave labour

Black slaves were bought and sold like property. They had to work hard. They were often cruelly treated or even killed by their owners.

Not everyone agreed with slavery, especially in the northern states. But the southern states did not want slavery to stop.

This photo was taken in 1863. It shows a slave being whipped for trying to escape. ➡

The Civil War

In 1860, the southern states broke away from the rest of the United States. From 1861 to 1865, the South fought the North in the Civil War.

The northern army fought mainly to keep the country together. But in 1862, President Abraham Lincoln made it clear that the war was also about ending slavery.

Black soldiers fought for the North in the Civil War. The South wanted to keep slavery but the government in the North was ready to end it.

Legal rights emerge

Three Amendments gave black people new rights:

January 1865 – the 13th Amendment made slavery illegal.

July 1868 – the 14th Amendment made people who had been slaves American citizens. It promised everyone equal protection under the law.

February 1870 – the 15th Amendment gave black American men the right to vote.

No equality

The Civil War ended in 1865. A change was made to the laws that govern the United States. This change was known as the 13th **Amendment**. It made slavery illegal (against the law).

Other Amendments followed that gave black Americans rights and freedoms. But they were still treated unfairly. They were sometimes killed just because they were black.

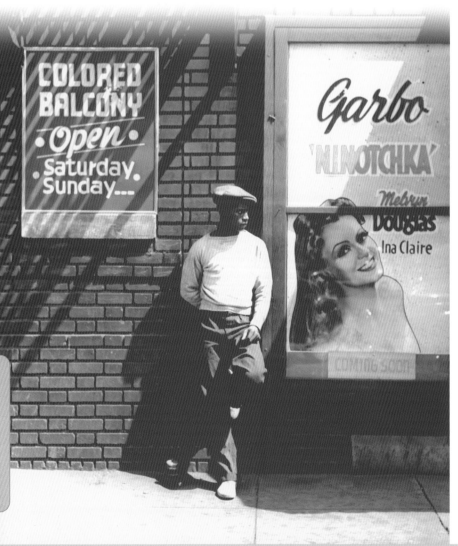

This is a cinema in Birmingham, Alabama, in 1940. Black people had to sit in a separate balcony at cinemas.

Word Bank   **Amendment**   change or addition to the laws that govern the United States

Jim Crow laws

In the 1890s, new laws were passed to keep black and white people apart. These were known as the **Jim Crow laws**. They stopped black people going to the same schools as whites. They made them use separate toilets and eat separately.

The struggle begins

There had always been brave black Americans who fought against this unfairness. But in the 1950s, many more joined in the fight. Their struggle was called the **civil rights movement**.

In the 1950s, black people from all over the United States began marching together to end **segregation**.

civil rights movement   effort made by black people and their supporters to try to get the same rights as white people

In 1955, Rosa Parks refused to give up her seat to a white man on a bus. Her action led to the first big protest of the **civil rights movement**.

Time for change

After Parks's arrest, most black people in Montgomery, Alabama, refused to use buses. Instead of using buses, they gave each other lifts, took taxis, or walked.

An empty bus drives by in Montgomery, Alabama. Meanwhile, people get into a car to ride to work together during the 1955 boycotts.

Word Bank boycott way of protesting that involves refusing to use something

Boycott!

This refusal was a form of protest called a **boycott**. The **protesters** said they would continue the boycott until black people got better treatment on buses.

The white community fought back. Police threatened taxi drivers and people sharing cars. They arrested some of the leaders of the boycott. But still no one used buses. Finally, in November 1956, **segregation** on public buses was made illegal.

In 1956 segregation on buses was made illegal. Rosa Parks is seen here taking another bus ride. This time she is sitting in the front.

An important leader

Martin Luther King Jr was one of the most important leaders of the civil rights struggle. He was a **Baptist minister**. King wanted to fight **injustice** without violence. He believed in peaceful protest.

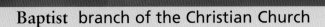

Baptist branch of the Christian Church

Throughout the United States, black children and white children went to separate schools. White children always had better schools and books than black children.

Fighting through the courts

Thurgood Marshall was a lawyer. He worked for the NAACP (see panel on the left). In 1954, Marshall went to court to try to stop **segregation** in schools.

The NAACP

The **National Association for the Advancement of Colored People (NAACP)** was formed in 1909. Its aim was to fight for equality. The NAACP used the court system to do this.

In 1954, George Hayes (left), Thurgood Marshall (middle), and James Nabrit (right) argued in court against segregation. They won.

Word Bank   segregation   keeping black people and white people separate

Before Marshall went to court, some **psychologists** made a study of black schoolchildren. They wanted to know how segregation made black children feel. The study showed that black children felt they were worth less than white children.

Separate is not equal

This study helped the judges make their decision. They decided that having separate schools for blacks and whites was not equality. The judges ordered schools to bring black and white children together.

The SCLC

In 1957, the **Southern Christian Leadership Conference (SCLC)** was formed. It aimed to get equality for black people through peaceful protests. The leader of the SCLC was Martin Luther King Jr.

The courts ordered segregation to stop. But some white schools still refused to let black pupils in. These children were turned away from a white school every day for two years.

psychologist someone who studies human behaviour

The "Little Rock Nine"

In 1954, the courts said that **segregation** in schools should stop. But many schools in the South still refused to take black students.

In 1957, nine brave black students decided to attend the all-white Central High School in Little Rock, Arkansas.

Three tries

The first time the "Little Rock Nine" tried to go to school, they could not get in. The governor of Arkansas had put armed guards around the school.

Through fighting segregation together, the "Little Rock Nine" became very close friends. Here they are studying together.

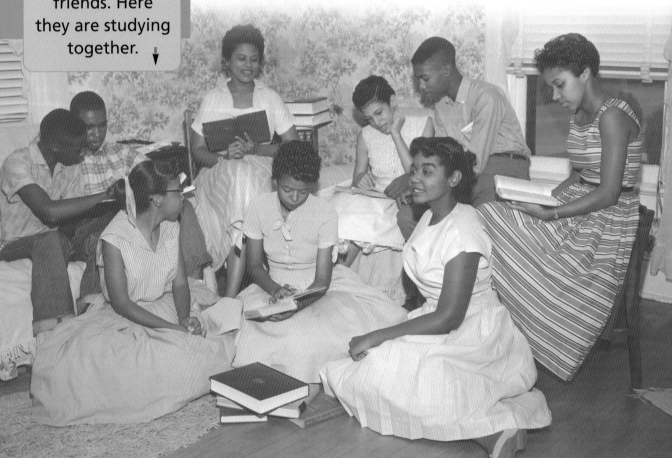

Word Bank desegregate when black and white people are no longer kept apart

The guards stopped them entering. The students tried to go to school a second time. But an angry crowd drove them away.

When the students tried a third time, US President Dwight Eisenhower sent soldiers to protect them. This time they got to their classes.

Success

The actions of the "Little Rock Nine" forced the Central High School to take black students. This led the way for other schools to do the same. Ending the separation of blacks and whites was called **desegregation**.

Desegregation timeline

1954 – The courts decide that segregation of schools is against the law.

1957 – The "Little Rock Nine" are admitted to Central High School in Little Rock, Arkansas.

1963 – In Alabama, Mississippi, and Louisiana, some black students attend elementary and secondary schools with whites.

1968 – The **Supreme Court** orders states to **desegregate** schools.

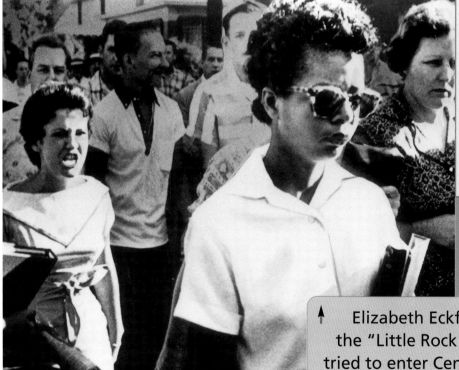

Elizabeth Eckford was one of the "Little Rock Nine". When she tried to enter Central High School in Little Rock, the crowd screamed at her and threatened to kill her.

Supreme Court top legal body in the United States

The "Greensboro Four"

Joseph McNeil was a student at university in Greensboro, North Carolina. On 1 February 1960, McNeil and three friends sat down at a lunch counter in Greensboro.

The lunch counter was for whites only. Black people had to get their food from the snack bar. But there were no seats at the snack bar.

This woman is stopping black people from entering a whites-only lunch counter. The picture was taken in Memphis, Tennessee, in 1961.

Word Bank sit-in peaceful protest where people sit down and refuse to leave

The waitress refused to serve them. But McNeil and his friends did not leave. They stayed and sat quietly. This kind of protest is known as a **sit-in**.

Success

The "Greensboro Four" returned the next day with other **protesters**. Sit-ins and other peaceful protests continued for five months.

Finally the store agreed to stop **segregation** at their lunch counters. This success led to other sit-ins throughout the country.

SNCC starts up

In April 1960, a group of students set up the **Student Non-Violent Coordinating Committee (SNCC,** called 'snick'). Snick organized sit-ins across the country.

Two of the "Greensboro Four" (left and second left), and two friends, sit in protest. They are at a whites-only lunch counter in Greensboro, North Carolina.

protester someone who shows disagreement through organized action, such as a march or a sit-in

Freedom rides

Segregation in interstate bus and train stations became illegal in 1960. But bus stations in the southern United States continued segregation. Blacks and whites had separate restaurants, waiting rooms, and toilets.

In February 1961, an organization called the **Congress of Racial Equality** (**CORE**) decided to test the law. They had a group of twelve volunteers. Some were black and some were white. These volunteers were called "freedom riders".

Making news
James Farmer was the founder of CORE. He remembered:

"We were counting on the bigots [people who are against anyone who is different] in the South to do our work for us... the government would have to respond if we created a situation that was headline news all over the world."

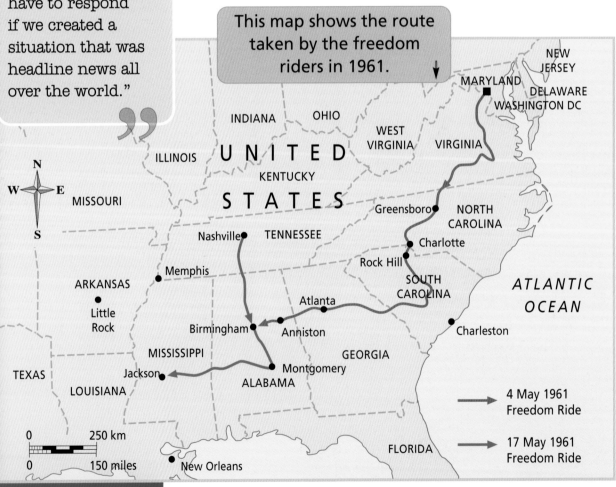

This map shows the route taken by the freedom riders in 1961.

Word Bank   interstate   travel from one state to another

Freedom riders would go on buses and into terminals in the South. They would travel from Washington DC to New Orleans. Black riders would use **facilities** meant for whites only. White riders would use facilities meant for blacks only.

Brave volunteers

The volunteers knew they might be arrested. They knew they would probably be attacked. But the riders would not use violence. They were scared, but they were determined.

Black and white freedom riders in 1961. They are sitting together in the "whites only" section of a bus station waiting room in 1961.

facilities places or equipment designed to provide a particular service or function, such as toilets, restaurants, or schools

Into the danger zone

On 4 May 1961, the freedom riders boarded their buses. Trouble started when the buses arrived in Birmingham, Alabama. An angry crowd waited at the terminal.

The police chief had kept police away. He did this so that angry whites could beat up the freedom riders. The white crowd did attack them. Some riders had to go to hospital.

These freedom riders in Alabama in 1961 watch as their bus burns.

Word Bank   civil rights freedoms within a country that all people should be granted

Never give up

At Anniston, Alabama, an angry crowd attacked another bus and beat up the riders. New volunteers continued the ride. More riders were beaten up at Montgomery, Alabama. Again, new volunteers took the places of those injured or arrested.

Freedom riders win

The riders' determination brought a lot of attention to the **civil rights** struggle. As a result, **segregated** bus stations disappeared in the South.

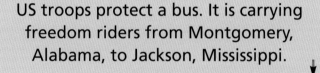

US troops protect a bus. It is carrying freedom riders from Montgomery, Alabama, to Jackson, Mississippi.

segregated when black people and white people are kept separate

DAYS OF BLOOD AND FIRE

In the 1950s and 1960s, black people in the southern United States feared the police. Many police officers did nothing when black people were beaten up. Often, the police themselves beat them up.

Time for action

There was particularly deep **racism** in Birmingham, Alabama. The city still had **segregation**. So in 1963, Martin Luther King Jr and other **civil rights** leaders went to Birmingham. Their aim was to stop segregation there.

Martin Luther King Jr, his wife, Coretta (center), and their son Martin Luther III, walk to a plane. This plane took King to Birmingham, Alabama.

Word Bank   racism hating a person because of his or her race or skin colour

Protests begin

Protesters held marches, **boycotts**, and **sit-ins** in Birmingham. They tried to get black people to **register** to vote. Hundreds were arrested. But every day more protesters took their places.

Locked up!

On 12 April 1963, Martin Luther King Jr was arrested for refusing to stop the protests. King wrote a letter to a newspaper while he was in jail (see panel on right). This letter is now famous.

Letter from jail

Some people thought Martin Luther King Jr should have stopped the protests. He wrote this letter from jail to explain why he did not:

"Perhaps it is easy for those who have never felt the stinging dart of segregation to say, 'Wait.' [But] when you are **humiliated** day in and day out . . . then you will understand why we find it difficult to wait."

Martin Luther King Jr in Birmingham jail in 1964.

humiliate make someone feel that they are not as good as everyone else; make them feel ashamed

Black children protest

In May 1963, Birmingham's black children and young adults decided to protest. On 2 May, 1,000 young people stayed away from school to march.

Dogs and violence

Police arrested more than 900 children on the first day. But the next day, more children showed up. The jails were full, so police set dogs on the children. Others were beaten by police or sprayed with water hoses.

Police set their dogs on a young adult **protester** during the riots in Alabama in 1963.

Word Bank   protester   someone who shows disagreement through organized action, such as a march or a sit-in

Soon, there were fights between blacks and whites. Business owners feared damage to their stores.

Fragile success

A plan to end **segregation** was agreed upon. Business owners also agreed to take on more black workers. Things seemed to settle down.

But then, a bomb exploded outside Martin Luther King Jr's hotel room. Some blamed the **Ku Klux Klan** (see side panel) for the attack. Black people rioted. The police then used force against the rioters.

The KKK

The Ku Klux Klan (KKK) is a secret organization. Its members are white people who believe whites are better than other races. The KKK has threatened and killed black people. This picture was taken in 1940. It shows KKK members at a meeting in their white robes.

segregation   keeping black people and white people separate

The president speaks up

On the night of 11 June 1963, US President John F. Kennedy went on television. He talked about introducing a new **civil rights** law.

Many black people watched the President that night. They hoped that he would support their struggle for equality. Myrlie Evers was one of them.

Working for the vote

Myrlie's husband was Medgar Evers. He worked for the **NAACP** in Mississippi. He was helping black

Barriers to voting

Any white person aged 21 or over could register to vote. But in the southern United States it was different for blacks. Before they could register to vote, they had to pass impossible tests or pay high taxes they could not afford.

President Kennedy talks to the nation by radio and television on 11 June 1963.

Word Bank   NAACP   one of the earliest civil rights organizations. The NAACP used the legal system to bring about change.

people to **register** to vote. Black men had been given the right to vote in 1870. But many states still used tricks and violence to stop them voting.

Evers is murdered

Not long after the President's broadcast, Medgar returned home late from work. Myrlie heard a gun shot. She ran to the door. Medgar had been shot and was crawling towards her. He died soon afterwards.

Medgar Evers received a hero's funeral. He is buried at Arlington National Cemetery in Washington DC.

register go through the process of qualifying to vote

March on Washington

The murder of Medgar Evers was a call for action. Many in the **civil rights movement** knew things needed to change quickly.

Black leaders planned a march on Washington DC. The leaders would then give speeches. They would try to raise support for President Kennedy's new **civil rights** law. This law would finally do away with the **Jim Crow laws**.

This is Martin Luther King Jr at the March on Washington in 1963.

Word Bank   civil rights movement effort made by black people and their supporters to try to get the same rights as white people

A peaceful message

On 28 August 1963, more than 200,000 people took part in the march. Thousands more watched it on television.

Speakers talked about **segregation**. They also talked about housing and jobs for black people.

The finest moment came when Martin Luther King Jr spoke. He made his famous "I have a dream" speech (see panel). Less than a year later the civil rights law was passed by **Congress**.

"I have a dream"

In this famous speech, Martin Luther King Jr spoke of the broken promise of equality for all. He spoke of his dream of a better future:

"I have a dream that one day this nation will rise up and live out the true meaning of its creed [beliefs] ... that all men are created equal."

During the march, thousands of people filled the area between the Lincoln Memorial and the Washington Monument in Washington DC.

Jim Crow laws laws supporting the segregation of black people and white people, named after a black character in a song

Innocent victims

The Washington march had raised many hopes. But the violence in the South continued. On Sunday, 15 September 1963, a bomb exploded in Birmingham, Alabama.

The bomb went off in the Sixteenth Street **Baptist** Church just before morning services. Four little girls were killed by the blast.

A man kneels after the Sixteenth Street Baptist Church bombing. He is praying for the children that died. ➔

Word Bank   Baptist branch of the Christian Church

Anger and riots

The bombing led to riots. Some angry black people attacked whites. They destroyed businesses owned by white people. Two more black children died.

Justice delayed

Four men were suspected of planting the bomb. But fourteen years passed before the first **suspect** was taken to court and found guilty. In 2001 and 2002, two others were found guilty. The fourth suspect was dead by this time. The three went to prison for life.

Too many bombs

Between 1957 and 1963 there were eighteen bombings in Birmingham. All of them were in black areas. It was years before anyone was convicted of the bombings. This was because many of those in charge did not care about violence against blacks.

Riots in Birmingham, Alabama, in 1963. The police used armoured trucks to try to keep the peace.

suspect   someone thought to be guilty of a crime

Pushing for votes

By the mid-1960s, **segregation** had ended. But many black people still could not vote. In Selma, Alabama, only one per cent of the black population was **registered** to vote.

On 7 March 1965, **protesters** began a march from Selma to Montgomery, the capital of Alabama. They wanted to present a list of complaints to Alabama's leaders.

Votes at last

Many think that the Selma marchers helped to get the Voting Rights Act passed. The Act was passed in 1965. It banned the tests that had stopped many blacks being able to vote (see page 26).

When the Selma marchers started out on 7 March and 9 March, they were faced by a wall of police.

Word Bank   register go through the process of qualifying to vote

Three marches

The state police stopped the marchers. They attacked the marchers with clubs and **tear gas**. Two days later, there was a second march. The marchers met again with police. The marchers knelt, prayed, then turned back.

On 21 March, a third march began. This time, the US government ordered police to protect the marchers. Twenty-five thousand people, both black and white, arrived in Montgomery. A few months later, a new voting rights law was passed.

Thousands of demonstrators joined Martin Luther King Jr (centre) on his march to Montgomery.

tear gas type of gas that makes your eyes fill with tears

March against fear

It was now easier for black Americans in the South to vote. But they still had to **register** their names. Many were frightened to do this.

On 5 March 1966, James Meredith began a march from Memphis, Tennessee, to Jackson, Mississippi. He wanted people to stop being afraid. He wanted them to register to vote.

Meredith is shot

On the second day of his march, Meredith was shot and wounded. Hundreds of people from **civil rights** organizations continued his march.

University riots

James Meredith (pictured below) had been the first black student at the University of Mississippi. His arrival there in 1962 caused riots that killed two people. It took more than 20,000 troops to calm things down.

On the second day of his march, James Meredith was shot. In this picture, he lies wounded on the ground.

Word Bank   SNCC civil rights group started by a younger generation of people

Meredith returns

Stokely Carmichael was the new leader of the **SNCC**. As the march moved through Mississippi, Carmichael made a famous speech about the need for "**black power**" (see panel right).

Meredith was well enough to join the march when it reached Jackson. By the end of the 22-day march, almost 4,000 black people had registered to vote.

Black power

Many young blacks were tired of King's way of doing things. The "black power" movement believed that the way to get equality was through black organizations and political groups. These would give blacks more strength and also pride in their race. Many also believed they should take what they wanted by force, if necessary.

Stokely Carmichael, head of the SNCC, was a very powerful speaker. ➡

black power movement formed by black people to gain equality and pride in their race through black organizations

A NEW APPROACH

Meredith's march in 1966 was the last time the major **civil rights** groups worked together. After that, many younger members joined new groups with different ideas about how to gain rights.

Many more riots

The mid-1960s was a time of trouble. Many riots started because of violence between police and blacks. New organizations were set up to fight for black rights.

The **Black Panther Party for Self-Defense** was formed in 1966. The Black Panthers carried weapons. They encouraged their members to defend themselves.

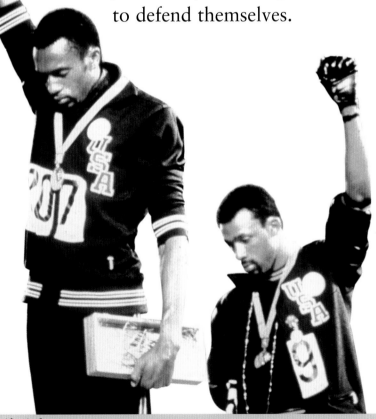

Word Bank civil rights freedoms within a country that all people should be granted

The **Nation of Islam** was another group that had become popular by this time. Many members believed that black people should live separately from whites.

Tired of violence

By the late 1960s, most Americans were tired of the violence. Americans began to think less about the struggle for civil rights.

Malcolm X was a strong black leader. He was a leader of the Nation of Islam but later left the group. He was murdered in 1965 by members of the Nation of Islam.

The Black Panthers

The Black Panthers (pictured above) believed in using violence, if necessary, to protect themselves. They wanted good housing for black people. They also wanted children to be taught black history in schools.

Nation of Islam black civil rights group. Many of its members favoured keeping black people apart from white people.

Focus on poverty

By the late 1960s, unfair laws had been changed. But many blacks were still living in terrible **poverty**. Poverty was hurting them as much as **segregation** once had.

The rubbish collectors

In 1968, Martin Luther King Jr decided to work to help the rubbish collectors in Memphis, Tennessee. They were paid very little and lived in awful conditions. King wanted better wages and better homes for black workers like them.

Martin Luther King Jr campaigned to reduce poverty amongst black families such as this one.

Word Bank   poverty   the state of being extremely poor

Shot dead

King made a speech in Memphis on 3 April 1968. He talked about threats on his life and his hope for better days. He said: "... I've seen the promised land. I may not get there with you. But I want you to know tonight, that we, as a people, will get to the promised land."

The next day, Martin Luther King Jr was shot dead outside his hotel room.

Set up?

James Earl Ray was arrested for King's murder. At first, Ray admitted killing King. But a few days later, he said he did not do it. Ray was found guilty and sent to prison. Some people believe that others were also involved in the shooting.

Martin Luther King Jr lies on the balcony of his hotel after being shot. **Civil rights** leaders point to where the gunshots came from.

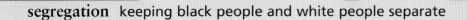

segregation keeping black people and white people separate

New attitudes

The 1950s and early 1960s were very important years for black people in the United States. Great changes happened during this time. Laws gave black people equal rights. But laws cannot control how white people feel towards black people.

Positive change

There is still **inequality** between blacks and whites. Over the years, the United States government has tried to make up for this.

Jobs such as teaching are now much more open to black people. Teachers today also teach **mixed-race** classes.

Word Bank mixed-race when people of different races are together

For example, today the law demands that schools and businesses must not **discriminate** against people based on their race.

Civil rights legacy

The **civil rights movement** has changed the way people think about others. People are able to learn and to change. If we continue to do this, we may see the day when no one is judged by the colour of their skin.

Today, children of all races live and learn side-by-side.

Secretary of State powerful head of the US Department of State that deals with foreign affairs

TIMELINE

1861

January The South breaks away from the United States of America.

April The Civil War begins.

1863

1 January President Abraham Lincoln legally frees slaves in the breakaway southern states.

1865

January The 13th **Amendment** makes slavery illegal.

May The Civil War ends in victory for the North.

1868

July The 14th Amendment makes those who had been slaves American citizens. It promises everyone equal protection under the law.

1870

February The 15th Amendment gives black men the right to vote.

1954

17 May The **Supreme Court** rules that **segregation** in public schools is unlawful.

1955

1 December Rosa Parks is arrested for refusing to give up her seat on a bus.

5 December The Montgomery Bus **boycott** begins.

1956

21 December Buses are **desegregated**.

1957

25 September The "Little Rock Nine" end segregation at Central High School.

1960

5 December The Supreme Court rules that segregation in **interstate** bus terminals is against the law.

1 February The "Greensboro Four" begin their **sit-in** at a **segregated** lunch counter.

1961

4 May Freedom rides begin.

1963

2 May A protest by black children begins in Birmingham, Alabama.

12 June Medgar Evers is murdered.

28 August The March on Washington is held.

15 September A bombing at the Sixteenth Street **Baptist** Church kills four little girls.

1964

2 July President Johnson signs the **Civil Rights** Act of 1964. This law makes segregation in public places illegal. It also makes it illegal to refuse to give someone a job because of his or her race.

1965

21 February Malcolm X is murdered.

7 March The Selma march begins.

10 August Congress passes the Voting Rights Act of 1965. This law bans testing as a way of stopping black people voting.

1966

5 June James Meredith starts his march.

1968

4 April Martin Luther King Jr is murdered.

Websites

We Shall Overcome
This website gives information on some historical places linked with the civil rights movement.
http://www.cr.nps.gov/nr/travel/civilrights

Civil Rights Movement Veterans
This website has information from, and about, people who took part in the civil rights movement.
http://www.crmvet.org/

The History Channel: Voices of Civil Rights
This is a collection of personal accounts of civil rights history. It includes video and sound recordings.
http://www.historychannel.com/classroom/voices/

Books

Black Stars of the Civil Rights Movement, by Jim Haskins (John Wiley & Sons, 2003)

Civil Rights in the USA, by Brendan January (Heinemann Library, 2003)

Martin Luther King, by Robert Jones (Usbourne Publishing, 2006)

DVD/VHS

Films about the civil rights movement are often aimed at an adult audience. Ask a parent or teacher before watching these.

Four Little Girls (1997)
A documentary about the bombing of an Alabama Baptist Church in 1963 that killed four black girls.

Mississippi Burning (1988)
The story of the investigation into the killing of three civil rights workers.

The Rosa Parks Story (2003)
A film about civil rights protester, Rosa Parks.

World wide web

To find out more about the civil rights movement you can search the Internet. Use keywords such as these:

- "freedom riders"
- civil rights + protest
- segregation + education

You can find your own keywords by using words from this book. The search tips below will help you find useful websites.

Most sites are aimed at adults. They can contain upsetting information and pictures. Make sure that you use well-known sites with correct information, such as those listed on page 44.

Search tips

There are billions of pages on the Internet. It can be difficult to find exactly what you are looking for. These tips will help you find useful websites more quickly:

- Know what you want to find out about.
- Use simple keywords.
- Use two to six keywords in a search.
- Only use names of people, places, or things.
- Put double quote marks around words that go together, for example "Jim Crow laws".

Where to search

Search engine
A search engine looks through millions of website pages. It lists all the sites that match the words in the search box. You will find the best matches are at the top of the list, on the first page.

Search directory
A person instead of a computer has sorted a search directory. You can search by keyword or subject and browse through the different sites. It is like looking through books on a library shelf.

GLOSSARY

Amendment change or addition to the laws that govern the United States

Baptist branch of the Christian Church

Black Panther Party for Self-Defense (Black Panthers) group formed in 1966 to protect blacks from police brutality. They believed in using violence, if necessary.

black power movement formed by black people to gain equality and pride in their race through black organizations

boycott way of protesting that involves refusing to use something

civil rights freedoms within a country that all people should be granted

civil rights movement effort made by black people and their supporters to try to get the same rights as white people

Congress law-making branch of the United States government

Congress of Racial Equality (CORE) civil rights organization that started sit-ins and freedom rides

desegregate when black and white people are no longer kept apart

desegregation ending the separation of black people and white people

discriminate treat someone differently from other people

facilities places or equipment designed to provide a particular service or function, such as toilets, restaurants, or schools

humiliate make someone feel that they are not as good as everyone else; make them feel ashamed

inequality when different groups of people do not get the same treatment or opportunities

injustice when people are treated unfairly

interstate travel from one state to another

Jim Crow laws laws supporting the segregation of black people and white people, named after a black character in a song

Ku Klux Klan (KKK) group of white people who believe that whites are better than all other races. During the civil rights movement, they terrorized and killed black people in the southern United States.

minister preacher in a church

mixed-race when people of different races are together

Nation of Islam black civil rights group. Many of its members favoured keeping black people apart from white people.

National Association for the Advancement of Colored People (NAACP) one of the earliest civil rights organizations. The NAACP used the legal system to bring about change.

poverty the state of being extremely poor

protester someone who shows disagreement through organized action, such as a march or a sit-in

psychologist someone who studies human behaviour

racism hating a person because of his or her race or skin colour

register go through the process of qualifying to vote

Secretary of State powerful head of the US Department of State that deals with foreign affairs

segregated when black people and white people are kept separate

segregation keeping black people and white people separate

sit-in peaceful protest where people sit down and refuse to leave

Southern Christian Leadership Conference (SCLC) civil rights group that pioneered the use of non-violent protests to bring about change

Student Non-Violent Coordinating Committee (SNCC) civil rights group started by a younger generation of people

Supreme Court top legal body in the United States

suspect someone thought to be guilty of a crime

tear gas type of gas that makes your eyes fill with tears

INDEX